Book 1

C Programming Success in a Day

BY SAM KEY

&

Book 2
Rails Programming
Professional Made Easy

BY SAM KEY

Book 1

C Programming Success in a Day

BY SAM KEY

Beginners' Guide To Fast, Easy And Efficient Learning Of C Programming

Table of Contents

Introduction

I want to thank you and congratulate you for purchasing the book, "C Programming Success in a Day – Beginners guide to fast, easy and efficient learning of Cc programming".

C. is one of the most popular and most used programming languages back then and today. Many expert developers have started with learning C in order to become knowledgeable in computer programming. In some grade schools and high schools, C programming is included on their curriculum.

If you are having doubts learning the language, do not. C is actually easy to learn. Compared to C++, C is much simpler and offer little. You do not need spend years to become a master of this language.

This book will tackle the basics when it comes to C. It will cover the basic functions you need in order to create programs that can produce output and accept input. Also, in the later chapters, you will learn how to make your program capable of simple thinking. And lastly, the last chapters will deal with teaching you how to create efficient programs with the help of loops.

Anyway, before you start programming using C, you need to get some things ready. First, you will need a compiler. A compiler is a program that will translate, compile, or convert your lines of code as an executable file. It means that, you will need a compiler for you to be able to run the program you have developed.

In case you are using this book as a supplementary source of information and you are taking a course of C, you might already have a compiler given to you by your instructor. If you are not, you can get one of the compilers that are available on the internet from MinGW.org.

You will also need a text editor. One of the best text editors you can use is Notepad++. It is free and can be downloadable from the internet. Also, it works well with MinGW's compiler.

In case you do not have time to configure or install those programs, you can go and get Microsoft's Visual C++ program. It contains all the things you need in order to practice developing programs using C or C++.

The content of this book was simplified in order for you to comprehend the ideas and practices in developing programs in C easily. Thanks again for purchasing this book. I hope you enjoy it!

Chapter 1: Hello World – the Basics

When coding a C program, you must start your code with the function 'main'. By the way, a function is a collection of action that aims to achieve one or more goals. For example, a vegetable peeler has one function, which is to remove a skin of a vegetable. The peeler is composed of parts (such as the blade and handle) that will aid you to perform its function. A C function is also composed of such components and they are the lines of codes within it.

Also, take note that in order to make your coding life easier, you will need to include some prebuilt headers or functions from your compiler.

To give you an idea on what C code looks like, check the sample below:

```c
#include <stdio.h>

int main()
{
    printf( "Hello World!\n" );

    getchar();

    return 0;
}
```

As you can see in the first line, the code used the #include directive to include the stdio.h in the program. In this case, the stdio.h will provide you with access to functions such as printf and getchar.

Main Declaration

After that, the second line contains int main(). This line tells the compiler that there exist a function named main. The int in the line indicates that the function main will return an integer or number.

Curly Braces

The next line contains a curly brace. In C programming, curly braces indicate the start and end of a code block or a function. A code block is a series of codes joined together in a series. When a function is called by the program, all the line of codes inside it will be executed.

Printf()

The printf function, which follows the opening curly brace is the first line of code in your main function or code block. Like the function main, the printf also have a code block within it, which is already created and included since you included <stdio.h> in your program. The function of printf is to print text into your program's display window.

Beside printf is the value or text that you want to print. It should be enclosed in parentheses to abide standard practice. The value that the code want to print is Hello World!. To make sure that printf to recognize that you want to print a string and display the text properly, it should be enclosed inside double quotation marks.

By the way, in programming, a single character is called a character while a sequence of characters is called a string.

Escape Sequence

You might have noticed that the sentence is followed by a \n. In C, \n means new line. Since your program will have problems if you put a new line or press enter on the value of the printf, it is best to use its text equivalent or the escape sequence of the new line.

By the way, the most common escape sequences used in C are:

\t = tab

\f = new page

\r = carriage return

\b = backspace

\v = vertical tab

Semicolons

After the last parenthesis, a semicolon follows. And if you look closer, almost every line of code ends with it. The reasoning behind that is that the semicolon acts as an indicator that it is the end of the line of code or command. Without it, the compiler will think that the following lines are included in the printf function. And if that happens, you will get a syntax error.

Getchar()

Next is the getchar() function. Its purpose is to receive user input from the keyboard. Many programmers use it as a method on pausing a program and letting the program wait for the user to interact with it before it executes the next line of code. To make the program move through after the getchar() function, the user must press the enter key.

In the example, if you compile or run it without getchar(), the program will open the display or the console, display the text, and then immediately close. Without the break provided by the getchar() function, the computer will execute those commands instantaneously. And the program will open and close so fast that you will not be able to even see the Hello World text in the display.

Return Statement

The last line of code in the function is return 0. The return statement is essential in function blocks. When the program reaches this part, the return statement will tell the program its value. Returning the 0 value will make the program interpret that the function or code block that was executed successfully.

And at the last line of the example is the closing curly brace. It signifies that the program has reached the end of the function.

It was not that not hard, was it? With that example alone, you can create simple programs that can display text. Play around with it a bit and familiarize yourself with C's basic syntax.

Chapter 2: Basic Input Output

After experimenting with what you learned in the previous chapter, you might have realized that it was not enough. It was boring. And just displaying what you typed in your program is a bit useless.

This time, this chapter will teach you how to create a program that can interact with the user. Check this code example:

```
#include <stdio.h>

int main()

{

        int number_container;

        printf( "Enter any number you want! " );

        scanf( "%d", &number_container );

        printf( "The number you entered is %d", number_container );

        getchar();

        return 0;

}
```

Variables

You might have noticed the int number_container part in the first line of the code block. int number_container is an example of variable declaration. To declare a variable in C, you must indicate the variable type first, and then the name of the variable name.

In the example, int was indicated as the variable or data type, which means the variable is an integer. There are other variable types in C such as float for floating-point numbers, char for characters, etc. Alternatively, the name number_container was indicated as the variable's name or identifier.

Variables are used to hold values throughout the program and code blocks. The programmer can let them assign a value to it and retrieve its value when it is needed.

For example:

int number_container;

number_container = 3;

printf ("The variables value is %d", number_container);

In that example, the first line declared that the program should create an integer variable named number_container. The second line assigned a value to the variable. And the third line makes the program print the text together with the value of the variable. When executed, the program will display:

The variables value is 3

You might have noticed the %d on the printf line on the example. The %d part indicates that the next value that will be printed will be an integer. Also, the quotation on the printf ended after %d. Why is that?

In order to print the value of a variable, it must be indicated with the double quotes. If you place double quotes on the variables name, the compiler will treat it as a literal string. If you do this:

int number_container;

number_container = 3;

printf ("The variables value is number_container");

The program will display:

The variables value is number_container

By the way, you can also use %i as a replacement for %d.

Assigning a value to a variable is simple. Just like in the previous example, just indicate the name of variable, follow it with an equal sign, and declare its value.

When creating variables, you must make sure that each variable will have unique names. Also, the variables should never have the same name as functions. In addition, you can declare multiple variables in one line by using commas. Below is an example:

int first_variable, second_variable, third_variable;

Those three variables will be int type variables. And again, never forget to place a semicolon after your declaration.

When assigning a value or retrieving the value of a variable, make sure that you declare its existence first. If not, the compiler will return an error since it will try to access something that does not exist yet.

Scanf()

In the first example in this chapter, you might have noticed the scanf function. The scanf function is also included in the <stdio.h>. Its purpose is to retrieve text user input from the user.

After the program displays the 'Enter any number you want' text, it will proceed in retrieving a number from the user. The cursor will be appear after the text since the new line escape character was no included in the printf.

The cursor will just blink and wait for the user to enter any characters or numbers. To let the program get the number the user typed and let it proceed to the next line of code, he must press the Enter key. Once he does that, the program will display the text 'The number you entered is' and the value of the number the user inputted a while ago.

To make the scanf function work, you must indicate the data type it needs to receive and the location of the variable where the value that scanf will get will be stored. In the example:

scanf("%d", &number_container);

The first part "%d" indicates that the scanf function must retrieve an integer. On the other hand, the next part indicates the location of the variable. You must have noticed the ampersand placed in front of the variable's name. The ampersand retrieves the location of the variable and tells it to the function.

Unlike the typical variable value assignment, scanf needs the location of the variable instead of its name alone. Due to that, without the ampersand, the function will not work.

Math or Arithmetic Operators

Aside from simply giving number variables with values by typing a number, you can assign values by using math operators. In C, you can add, subtract, multiply, and divide numbers and assign the result to variables directly. For example:

int sum;

sum = 1 + 2;

If you print the value of sum, it will return a 3, which is the result of the addition of 1 and 2. By the way, the + sign is for addition, - for subtraction, * for multiplication, and / for division.

With the things you have learned as of now, you can create a simple calculator program. Below is an example code:

```c
#include <stdio.h>

int main()

{

        int first_addend, second_addend, sum;

        printf( "Enter the first addend! " );

        scanf( "%d", &first_addend );

        printf( "\nEnter the second addend! " );

        scanf( "%d", &second_addend );

        sum = first_addend + second_addend;

        printf( "The sum of the two numbers is %d", sum );

        getchar();

        return 0;

}
```

Chapter 3: Conditional Statements

The calculator program seems nice, is it not? However, the previous example limits you on creating programs that only uses one operation, which is a bit disappointing. Well, in this chapter, you can improve that program with the help of if or conditional statements. And of course, learning this will improve your overall programming skills. This is the part where you will be able to make your program 'think'.

'If' statements can allow you to create branches in your code blocks. Using them allows you to let the program think and perform specific functions or actions depending on certain variables and situations. Below is an example:

```c
#include <stdio.h>

int main()

{

        int some_number;

        printf( "Welcome to Guess the Magic Number program. \n" );

        printf( "Guess the magic number to win. \n" );

        printf( "Type the magic number and press Enter: " );

        scanf( "%d", &some_number );

        if ( some_number == 3 ) {

                printf( "You guessed the right number! " );

        }

        getchar();

        return 0;

}
```

In the example, the if statement checked if the value of the variable some_number is equal to number 3. In case the user entered the number 3 on the program, the comparison between the variable some_number and three will return TRUE since the value of some_number 3 is true. Since the value that the if statement received was TRUE, then it will process the code block below it. And the result will be:

You guessed the right number!

If the user input a number other than three, the comparison will return a FALSE value. If that happens, the program will skip the code block in the if statement and proceed to the next line of code after the if statement's code block.

By the way, remember that you need to use the curly braces to enclosed the functions that you want to happen in case your if statement returns TRUE. Also, when inserting if statement, you do not need to place a semicolon after the if statement or its code block's closing curly brace. However, you will still need to place semicolons on the functions inside the code blocks of your if statements.

TRUE and FALSE

The if statement will always return TRUE if the condition is satisfied. For example, the condition in the if statement is 10 > 2. Since 10 is greater than 2, then it is true. On the other hand, the if statement will always return FALSE if the condition is not satisfied. For example, the condition in the if statement is 5 < 5. Since 5 is not less than 5, then the statement will return a FALSE.

Note that if statements only return two results: TRUE and FALSE. In computer programming, the number equivalent to TRUE is any nonzero number. In some cases, it is only the number 1. On the other hand, the number equivalent of FALSE is zero.

Operators

Also, if statements use comparison, Boolean, or relational and logical operators. Some of those operators are:

== – equal to

!= – not equal to

> – greater than

< – less than

>= – greater than or equal to

<= – less than or equal to

Else Statement

There will be times that you would want your program to do something else in case your if statement return FALSE. And that is what the else statement is for. Check the example below:

```
#include <stdio.h>

int main()

{

        int some_number;

        printf( "Welcome to Guess the Magic Number program. \n" );

        printf( "Guess the magic number to win. \n" );

        printf( "Type the magic number and press Enter: " );

        scanf( "%d", &some_number );

        if ( some_number == 3 ) {

                printf( "You guessed the right number! " );
```

```
    }

    else {

            printf( "Sorry. That is the wrong number" );

    }

    getchar();

    return 0;

}
```

If ever the if statement returns FALSE, the program will skip next to the else statement immediately. And since the if statement returns FALSE, it will immediately process the code block inside the else statement.

For example, if the number the user inputted on the program is 2, the if statement will return a FALSE. Due to that, the else statement will be processed, and the program will display:

Sorry. That is the wrong number

On the other hand, if the if statement returns TRUE, it will process the if statement's code block, but it will bypass all the succeeding else statements below it.

Else If

If you want more conditional checks on your program, you will need to take advantage of else if. Else if is a combination of the if and else statement. It will act like an else statement, but instead of letting the program execute the code block below it, it will perform another check as if it was an if statement. Below is an example:

19

```c
#include <stdio.h>

int main()

{

    int some_number;

    printf( "Welcome to Guess the Magic Number program. \n" );

    printf( "Guess the magic number to win. \n" );

    printf( "Type the magic number and press Enter: " );

    scanf( "%d", &some_number );

    if ( some_number == 3 ) {

        printf( "You guessed the right number! " );

    }

    else if ( some_number > 3 ){

        printf( "Your guess is too high!" );

    }

    else {

        printf( "Your guess is too low!" );

    }

    getchar();

    return 0;

}
```

In case the if statement returns FALSE, the program will evaluate the else if statement. If it returns TRUE, it will execute its code block and ignore the following else statements. However, if it is FALSE, it will proceed on the last else statement, and execute its code block. And just like before, if the first if statement returns true, it will disregard the following else and else if statements.

In the example, if the user inputs 3, he will get the You guessed the right number message. If the user inputs 4 or higher, he will get the Your guess is too high message. And if he inputs any other number, he will get a Your guess is too low message since any number aside from 3 and 4 or higher is automatically lower than 3.

With the knowledge you have now, you can upgrade the example calculator program to handle different operations. Look at the example and study it:

```
#include <stdio.h>

int main()

{
        int first_number, second_number, result, operation;

        printf( "Enter the first number: " );

        scanf( "%d", &first_number );

        printf( "\nEnter the second number: " );

        scanf( "%d", &second_number );

        printf ( "What operation would you like to use? \n" );

        printf ( "Enter 1 for addition. \n" );

        printf ( "Enter 2 for subtraction. \n" );

        printf ( "Enter 3 for multiplication. \n" );

        printf ( "Enter 4 for division. \n" );
```

```c
        scanf( "%d", &operation );

        if ( operation == 1 ) {

                result = first_number + second_number;

                printf( "The sum is %d", result );

        }

        else if ( operation == 2 ){

                result = first_number - second_number;

                printf( "The difference is %d", result );

        }

        else if ( operation == 3 ){

                result = first_number * second_number;

                printf( "The product is %d", result );

        }

        else if ( operation == 4 ){

                result = first_number / second_number;

                printf( "The quotient is %d", result );

        }

        else {

                printf( "You have entered an invalid choice." );

        }

        getchar();

        return 0;

}
```

Chapter 4: Looping in C

The calculator's code is getting better, right? As of now, it is possible that you are thinking about the programs that you could create with the usage of the conditional statements.

However, as you might have noticed in the calculator program, it seems kind of painstaking to use. You get to only choose one operation every time you run the program. When the calculation ends, the program closes. And that can be very annoying and unproductive.

To solve that, you must create loops in the program. Loops are designed to let the program execute some of the functions inside its code blocks. It effectively eliminates the need to write some same line of codes. It saves the time of the programmer and it makes the program run more efficiently.

There are four different ways in creating a loop in C. In this chapter, two of the only used and simplest loop method will be discussed. To grasp the concept of looping faster, check the example below:

```c
#include <stdio.h>

int main()

{

        int some_number;

        int guess_result;

        guess_result = 0;


        printf( "Welcome to Guess the Magic Number program. \n" );

        printf( "Guess the magic number to win. \n" );

        printf( "You have unlimited chances to guess the number. \n" );
```

```
while ( guess_result == 0 ) {

        printf( "Guess the magic number: " );

        scanf( "%d", &some_number );

        if ( some_number == 3 ) {

                printf( "You guessed the right number! \n" );

                guess_result = 1;

        }

        else if ( some_number > 3 ){

                printf( "Your guess is too high! \n" );

                guess_result = 0;

        }

        else {

                printf( "Your guess is too low! \n" );

                guess_result = 0;

        }

}

printf( "Thank you for playing. Press Enter to exit this program." );

getchar();

return 0;

}
```

While Loop

In this example, the while loop function was used. The while loop allows the program to execute the code block inside it as long as the condition is met or the argument in it returns TRUE. It is one of the simplest loop function in C. In the example, the condition that the while loop requires is that the guess_result variable should be equal to 0.

As you can see, in order to make sure that the while loop will start, the value of the guess_result variable was set to 0.

If you have not noticed it yet, you can actually nest code blocks within code blocks. In this case, the code block of the if and else statements were inside the code block of the while statement.

Anyway, every time the code reaches the end of the while statement and the guess_result variable is set to 0, it will repeat itself. And to make sure that the program or user experience getting stuck into an infinite loop, a safety measure was included.

In the example, the only way to escape the loop is to guess the magic number. If the if statement within the while code block was satisfied, its code block will run. In that code block, a line of code sets the variable guess_result's value to 1. This effectively prevent the while loop from running once more since the guess_result's value is not 0 anymore, which makes the statement return a FALSE.

Once that happens, the code block of the while loop and the code blocks inside it will be ignored. It will skip to the last printf line, which will display the end program message 'Thank you for playing. Press Enter to exit this program'.

For Loop

The for loop is one of the most handy looping function in C. And its main use is to perform repetitive commands on a set number of times. Below is an example of its use:

```c
#include <stdio.h>

int main()

{

    int some_number;

    int x;

    int y;


    printf( "Welcome to Guess the Magic Number program. \n" );

    printf( "Guess the magic number to win. \n" );

    printf( "You have only three chance of guessing. \n" );

    printf( "If you do not get the correct answer after guessing three times. \n"
    );

    printf( "This program will be terminated. \n" );


    for (x = 0; x < 3; x++) {

        y = 3 − x;

        printf( "The number of guesses that you have left is: %d", y );

        printf( "\nGuess the magic number: " );

        scanf( "%d", &some_number );

        if ( some_number == 3 ) {

            printf( "You guessed the right number! \n" );

            x = 4;

        }

        else if ( some_number > 3 ){
```

```
        printf( "Your guess is too high! \n " );

    }

    else {

        printf( "Your guess is too low! \n " );

    }

}

printf( "Press the Enter button to close this program. \n" );

getchar();

getchar();

return 0;

}
```

The for statement's argument section or part requires three things. First, the initial value of the variable that will be used. In this case, the example declared that x = 0. Second, the condition. In the example, the for loop will run until x has a value lower than 3. Third, the variable update line. Every time the for loop loops, the variable update will be executed. In this case, the variable update that will be triggered is x++.

Increment and Decrement Operators

By the way, x++ is a variable assignment line. The x is the variable and the ++ is an increment operator. The function of an increment operator is to add 1 to the variable where it was placed. In this case, every time the program reads x++, the program will add 1 to the variable x. If x has a value of 10, the increment operator will change variable x's value to 11.

On the other hand, you can also use the decrement operator instead of the increment operator. The decrement operator is done by place -- next to a variable. Unlike the increment operator, the decrement subtracts 1 to its operand.

27

Just like the while loop, the for loop will run as long as its condition returns TRUE. However, the for loop has a built in safety measure and variable declaration. You do not need to declare the value needed for its condition outside the statement. And the safety measure to prevent infinite loop is the variable update. However, it does not mean that it will be automatically immune to infinite loops. Poor programming can lead to it. For example:

```
for (x = 1; x > 1; x++) {

        /* Insert Code Block Here */

}
```

In this example, the for loop will enter into an infinite loop unless a proper means of escape from the loop is coded inside its code block.

The structure of the for loop example is almost the same with while loop. The only difference is that the program is set to loop for only three times. In this case, it only allows the user to guess three times or until the value of variable x does not reach 3 or higher.

Every time the user guesses wrong, the value of x is incremented, which puts the loop closer in ending. However, in case the user guesses right, the code block of the if statement assigns a value higher than 3 to variable x in order to escape the loop and end the program.

Conclusion

Thank you again for purchasing this book!

I hope this book was able to help you to learn the basics of C programming. The next step is to learn the other looping methods, pointers, arrays, strings, command line arguments, recursion, and binary trees.

Finally, if you enjoyed this book, please take the time to share your thoughts and post a review on Amazon. We do our best to reach out to readers and provide the best value we can. Your positive review will help us achieve that. It'd be greatly appreciated!
Thank you and good luck!

Book 2
Rails Programming
Professional Made Easy

BY SAM KEY

Expert Rails Programming Success In A Day For Any Computer User!

Table of Contents

Introduction

I want to thank you and congratulate you for purchasing the book, "insert book title here Professional Rails Programming Made Easy: Expert Rails Programming Success In A Day For Any Computer User!"

This book contains proven steps and strategies on how to learn the program Ruby on Rails and immediately create an application by applying the rudiments of this platform.

Rails is one of the newest and most popular platforms. Thanks to the growth of Internet, this platform has been targeting audiences that are quite interested in creating stable web designs. If your work involves the Internet and you want to implement ideas that would help you launch projects online, you would definitely want to learn how to code using this program. Within this book are everything that you need to learn from installing the platform, getting the basics and making sure that you are ready to rock any programmer's boat.

Thanks again for purchasing this book. I hope you enjoy it!

Chapter 1 Why Rails Matters

If you are a computer programmer, the Ruby on Rails platform would probably the next program that you have to learn how to use. It is also worth looking into if your work is largely based on design, and you want to try something current to make websites easy to manipulate and beautiful. It could also be the platform that would launch your career or create leverage for yourself at the office. Yes, this platform could be your trump card to your next promotion, or that awesome site that you have in mind.

What Rails Can Do For You

If you are wondering what good this program can do for most computer users, then here are the awesome things that you can get out of the platform.

1. Get to Code

Coding is not rocket science, and if you are using Ruby, you probably would not even feel that you are using a programming language. You would want to learn to code to retain what you are going to experience with the platform, so take the time to study anyway.

If you are getting into Rails, you do not need to be a Computer Science major. If you are a businessman who has a great idea for a web app and you want to try coding it yourself, then this platform may be your best bet.

2. Get to Code Better

Sometimes it is not about arguing what is the best platform out there and get drunk arguing which is the best among Python, Java, PHP, or Ruby. If you already know other programming languages, you would need to still keep up with the times and learn some new tricks. Ruby on Rails provides that opportunity.

3. Get to Code Faster

RoR is a beautiful platform that allows you to write shorter codes, and it has a great set of features for exception handling which makes it really easy to spot and handle possible errors. You also would not need to still maintain the usual reference counts in your extension libraries. You also get awesome support using Ruby from C, which gives you better handle when you want to write C extensions. RoR makes any programmer productive because it is opinionated and it gives guesses on how you can probably code something in the best way possible. The Don't Repeat Yourself (DRY) Principle of RoR also makes you skip the usual coding process of writing something again and again, which often makes the code long, complex, and difficult to debug. That means that at the end of the project, you get to look at your code and have a better grasp of what happened there.

4. Understand How Twitter Works

Yes, Twitter is created using RoR, and if you are an SEO specialist, a web designer, or simply a tech geek, knowing how this social media platform is done would definitely help you out. You would also discover that a lot of the hot new websites today are built on this platform.

5. Learn a Platform with a Great Community

RoR is relatively young compared to other programming languages, and for that reason, it has a very active and collaborative community. You definitely would get to hang out with several other developers and would probably build something together. Doing that is always good for your résumé.

6. It works with all operating systems and offers threading that is independent from the operating system. That means that is also very portable, and would even work on a computer that runs on Windows 95.

If these perks sound great, then it's time to get started with a Rails project!

Chapter 2 Getting Started

If you want to learn how to use Rails, then you would need to first have the following:

1. Ruby – choose the language version that is 1.9.3, or later. You can download it by visiting ruby-lang.org.

2. RubyGems packaging system – it is typically installed with Ruby that has versions 1.9 or newer.

3. Installed SQLite3 Database

Rails, as you probably figured out, is a framework dedicated to web application development written in the language of Ruby. That means that you would want to learn a little bit of Ruby coding in order to eliminate any difficulty in jumping into Rails. If you have a browser open, you can get great help in practicing Ruby codes by logging in to tryruby.org, which features a great interactive web tutorial. Try it out first to get the hang out of coding with Ruby.

If you do not have any working SQLite 3 yet, you can find it at sqlite.org. You can also get installation instructions there.

Installing Rails

1. Run the Rails installer (for Windows and Mac users) or the Tokaido (Mac OS X users)

2. Check out the version of the installed Ruby on your computer by running the Run command on Start menu and then typing cmd on the prompt (Windows). If you are running on Mac OS X, launch Terminal.app.

Key in "$ ruby –v" (no captions). After you hit Enter, you will see the Ruby version installed

3. Check out the version of SQLite3 installed by typing "$ sqlite3 –version".

4. After Rails installation, type in "$ rails –version" on Terminal.app or at the command prompt. If it says something similar to Rails 4.2.0, then you are good to go.

A Note on the $ sign

The $ sign would be used here in this book to look like the terminal prompt where you would type your code after. If you are using Windows for the Rails platform, you would see something like this: c:\source_code> .

Chapter 3 Create Your First Project

Here's something that most web developers are raving about Rails: it comes with generators, or scripts that are made to make development a lot easier by making all things that you need to get started on a particular project. Among these scripts is the new application generator, which gives you the foundation you need for a new Rails app so you do not have to write one yourself. Now that allows you to jump right into your code!

Since you are most likely to build a website or an API (application program interface), you would want to start coding a blog application. To start, launch a terminal and go to any directory where you can create files. On the prompt, type "$ rails new blog."

After you hit Enter, Rails will start making an application called Blog in the directory. It will also start making gem dependencies that you already have in your Gemfile bundle install.

Now, go to where your blog app is by typing in "$ cd blog".

What's in There?

Once you get into the directory, you will find a number of files that Rails have already installed by default. If you are not quite sure about what these files are for, here's a quick rundown of the file or folder functions:

1. app/ - this has the models, helpers, mailers, assets, and controllers for the app you just created. You'll be looking more at this folder later.

2. bin/ - this has the script that you will use to run the app. Also, this has other scripts that you will be using to deploy, setup, or run the application you are going to create.

3. config/ - this allows you to tweak the app's database, routes, etc.

4. config.ru – this is the configuration that will be used by Rack-based servers to run the app.

5. db/ - this would contain your database and database migrations

6. Gemfile, Gemfile.lock – these would allow you to tell the program what sort of gem dependencies you are going to need for the app you're building.

7. lib/ - contains the extended modules needed for the app

8. lib – contains the app's log files

9. public/ – this would be the sole folder that other people could see. It would be containing all your compiled assets and created static files.

10. Rakefile – this would be the one file that would locate and load tasks that can be set to run from the command line. You can add tasks that you would prefer to use later on by adding the files needed to the lib/tasks directory

11. README.rdoc – just like readme's function, this would be a brief document that would tell other people how your app works, how to set it up, etc.

12. test/ - these would contain all your unit tests and all the things that you are going to need for testing.

13. tmp/ - this would hold all temporary files

14. vendor/ - this would contain all your third-party codes and would also contain all vendored gems.

Now, if you are seeing all these in the app directory you just made, then you are ready to create little bits and pieces that you would be adding up later to make a real blog app!

Firing Up the Web Server

Since you already have the barebones of your blog application, you would want to set up how the app is going to be launched on the internet. To start a web server go to the directory where blog is located, and then type "$ bin/rails server".

Important note:

You would need to have a JavaScript runtime available in your computer if you want to use asset compression for JavaScript or if you want to compile a CoffeeScript. Otherwise, you would expect to see an execjs error when you attempt to compile these assets. If you want to look at all the supported runtimes, you can go to github.com/sstephenson/execjs#readme.

If you are successful, what you just did would launch WEBrick, which is the server that Ruby apps use by default. You can see what's happening so far in your app by firing up a web browser and typing http://localhost:3000. Now, since you have done nothing much, you would be seeing the Rails default page. It will tell you that you are currently in development mode. You also do not need to constantly require the server to look at the changes that you have made – any changes will be automatically picked up and seen. Also keep in mind that if you managed to see this "Welcome Aboard" thing, you are sure that you created an app that is configured correctly. If you want to find out the app's environment, click on "About your application's environment" link.

Got everything right so far? Let's move on to making something other people can read.

Chapter 4 Say "Hello There!"

If you want to make Rails learn how to say Hi to other people, you would need the following:

1. A controller

The purpose of a controller is to allow your program to receive any requests. When you route, you enable Rails to decide which of the controllers you set up will receive which types of requests. That may also mean that there would be different routes leading to the controller, which would be triggered by specific actions. An action is required in order to collect any information needed in order to send it to a view

2. A view

This thing's main purpose is to enable Rails to display the information made available to the action and display it in a format that other people can read. There are different view templates that are already available and coded using eRuby, which can be used in request cycles before it the information is sent to anyone who wants to look at this information.

Got it? Good. Now, to setup your welcome page, you need to generate a controller and then name it "welcome" using an action named "index". Your code will look like this:

$ bin/rails generate controller welcome index

Now, Rails will be creating a bunch of files plus a route for you to use. When Rails is done with that, you will see this:

```
      create  app/controllers/welcome_controller.rb
       route  get 'welcome/index'
      invoke  erb
      create   app/views/welcome
      create   app/views/welcome/index.html.erb
      invoke  test_unit
      create   test/controllers/welcome_controller_test.rb
      invoke  helper
      create  app/helpers/welcome_helper.rb
      invoke  assets
      invoke   coffee
      create      app/assets/javascripts/welcome.js.coffee
      invoke   scss
      create      app/assets/stylesheets/welcome.css.scss
```

If you want to view where the course of your controller is, go to app/controllers/welcome_controller.rb. If you want to look at the view, you can find it at app/views/welcome/index.html.erb.

Here comes the fun part. Pull up a text editor and open app/views/welcome/index.html.erb there. Clear all the codes you see there, and replace it with this:

```
      <h1>Hello Rails!</h1>
```

Programming #11:C Programming Success in a Day & Rails Programming Professional Made Easy

After doing so, you have successfully informed Rails that you want "Hello Rails!" to appear. That means that it is also the greeting that you want to see when you go to http://localhost:3000, which is still displaying "Welcome aboard".
Create the App's Home Page
The next thing that you need to do is to tell Rails where the home page is. To do that, pull up your text editor again and open config/routes.rb. You should see something like this:

```
        Rails.application.routes.draw do
    get 'welcome/index'

    # The priority is based upon order of creation:
    # first created -> highest priority.
    #
    # You can have the root of your site routed with "root"
    # root 'welcome#index'
    #
    # ...
```

Those lines represent the routing file which tells Rails how to link requests to specific actions and controllers. Now, find the line "root 'welcome#index'" and uncomment it. When you get back to http://localhost:3000, you will see that it now displays Hello Rails!

Chapter 5 Let's Do Something More

Now that you have figured out how to make a controller, a view, and an action, it's time to create a new resource. A resource is something that groups together similar objects the same way you group people, plants, and animals. To make items for resources, you use the CRUD method (create, read, update, destroy).

Rails make it easy for you to build websites because it already comes with a method for resources that it can use for making a REST resource. REST, or Representational State Transfer is known as the web's architectural structure which is used to design all applications that use a network, and instead of using rather complex operations to link two machines, you can use HTTP to make machines communicate. That means that in a lot of ways, the Internet is based on a RESTful design.

Now, following the project you are creating, pull up config/routes.rb and make sure it's going to look like this:

Rails.application.routes.draw do

    resources :articles

    root 'welcome#index'
    end

If you are going to look at the rake routes, you will notice that Rails has already made routes for all actions involving REST. It is going to look like this:

```
$ bin/rake routes
      Prefix Verb   URI Pattern              Controller#Action
     articles GET   /articles(.:format)        articles#index
          POST  /articles(.:format)        articles#create
 new_article GET   /articles/new(.:format)    articles#new
edit_article GET   /articles/:id/edit(.:format) articles#edit
    article GET   /articles/:id(.:format)     articles#show
         PATCH /articles/:id(.:format)     articles#update
         PUT   /articles/:id(.:format)    articles#update
         DELETE /articles/:id(.:format)     articles#destroy
     root GET   /                    welcome#index
```

Chapter 6 Creating Article Title

This part would be the creating and reading part of CRUD, where you would put in a location where you would be placing articles for the blog you're building. In order to do so, you can create an ArticlesController by running this code:

$ bin/rails g controller articles

Now, you need to manually place an action inside the controller that you just created. Go to app/controllers/articles_controller.rb and pull up the class ArticlesController. Edit it to look like this:

class ArticlesController < ApplicationController
  def new
  end
end

You now have to create a template that Rails would be able to view. In order to create a title for the article that you want to display, pull up app/views/articles/new.html.erb and make a new file there. Type the following:

<h1>New Article</h1>

What did just happen? Check out http://localhost:3000/articles/new and you will see that the page now has a title! You will now want to create a template that will look like a form that you can fill up to write your articles in online.

Chapter 7 Creating the Form

Pull up app/views/articles/new.html.erb and then add this code:

```
<%= form_for :article do |f| %>
<p>
 <%= f.label :title %><br>
 <%= f.text_field :title %>
</p>

<p>
 <%= f.label :text %><br>
 <%= f.text_area :text %>
</p>

<p>
 <%= f.submit %>
</p>
<% end %>
```

You will see that you have just created a form that has a space for the article title text, submit button, and it comes with boxes too! That is the function of the code form_for. You will realize that when you submit an article you are going to create, it needs to be done in another URL and then the entire text should then go somewhere else. Edit app/views/articles/new.html.erb by finding the form_for line and make it look like this:

```
<%= form_for :article, url: articles_path do |f| %>
```

In Rails, the action "create" does the job of making new forms for submissions, and therefore, your form should be working towards this action. You would notice that when you try to submit an article, you would see an error there. In order to make it work, you need to make a "create action" within the ArticlesController.

Create the Article

In order to get rid of this error, you need to edit the ArticlesController class found in app/controllers/articles_controller.rb. It should look like this:

```
class ArticlesController < ApplicationController
    def new
    end

    def create
    end
end
```

Once that is done, the controller should now be able to save the article to the database. Now, you would need to set the parameters of actions done by controllers. Now, make the ending of the above lines to look like this instead:

```
def create
  render plain: params[:article].inspect
end
```

Now that should make the error go away. Try refreshing the page to see what happened.

Make the Model

Rails already provide a generator that would be used by your project to launch a model. To order Rails to start generating one, run this on the terminal:

$ bin/rails generate model Article title:string text:text

What just happened is that you told Rails that you are requiring an Article model that has a title and a text that are attributed to separate strings. You would see that the platform made up a lot of files, but you would be most interested in db/migrate/20140120191729_create_articles.rb which contains your blog's database.

Now, you would want to run a migration, which you can do with a single line of code:

$ bin/rake db:migrate

What Rails would do is that it would be executing this command which means that it made the Articles Table:

```
==                          CreateArticles:              migrating
=================================================
-- create_table(:articles)
  -> 0.0019s
==                 CreateArticles:          migrated        (0.0020s)
=======================================
```

Chapter 8 Save Your Data

Pull up app/controllers/articles_controller.rb and edit the "create" action into this:

```
def create
  @article = Article.new(params[:article])

  @article.save
  redirect_to @article
end
```

You're almost able to create an article! However, when you refresh the page, you would see a Forbidden Attributes Error, and would point you at the line @article – Article.new(params[:article]). The reason Rails is giving you a hard time is because it wants you to tell what parameters should be in your controller actions. That allows your program to be secure once you run it, and prevent it from assigning wrong controller parameters which can make your entire coded program crash.

To fix this, edit out the highlighted line in the error you just saw and change it into:

```
@article = Article.new(params.require(:article).permit(:title, :text))
```

Show Your Work

In order to make the page display your article, you can make use of the "show" action by adding it to app/controllers/articles_controller.rb. Add these following lines:

```
class ArticlesController < ApplicationController
  def show
    @article = Article.find(params[:id])
  end

  def new
  end
```

Now let's add some style. Create a new file named app/views/articles/show.html.erb and put in the following lines:

```
<p>
  <strong>Title:</strong>
  <%= @article.title %>
</p>

<p>
  <strong>Text:</strong>
  <%= @article.text %>
</p>
```

Refresh http://localhost:3000/articles/new and then you will see that you can create articles and display them!

Chapter 9 Make Your Articles Neat

Find a way to list all the articles that you are going to create in order to have an organized database. To do that, pull up app/controllers/articles_controller.rb and add the following lines to create a control.

```
class ArticlesController < ApplicationController
  def index
    @articles = Article.all
  end

  def show
    @article = Article.find(params[:id])
  end

  def new
  end
```

Now, to add a view, pull up app/views/articles/index.html.erb and then add the following lines:

```
<h1>Article List</h1>

<table>
 <tr>
  <th>Title</th>
  <th>Text</th>
 </tr>

 <% @articles.each do |article| %>
  <tr>
   <td><%= article.title %></td>
   <td><%= article.text %></td>
  </tr>
 <% end %>
</table>
```

Head over to http://localhost:3000/articles and you will see all the articles that you have made so far.

Tidy Up Some More with Links

You definitely need to create links for the articles that you have created so your readers can pull them up easily. To add links, open app/views/welcome/index.html.erb and then change it to look like this:

```
<h1>Hello, Rails!</h1>
<%= link_to 'My Blog', controller: 'articles' %>
```

Now, what if you want to add a link that would allow you to write a new article right away? All you need to do is to add the following lines to app/views/articles/index.html.erb to have a New Article link:

```
%= link_to 'New article', new_article_path %>
```

If you want to create a link to go back to where you were previously, add the following lines to the same file:

```
<%= form_for :article, url: articles_path do |f| %>
 ...
<% end %>

<%= link_to 'Back', articles_path %>
```

Chapter 10 Create Some Rules, Too

When you are creating a blog program, you do not want your users to accidentally submit a blank page, and then just land right back where they were without knowing what they did. Rails can help you make sure that doesn't happen by editing the app/models/article.rb file to look like this:

```
class Article < ActiveRecord::Base
  validates :title, presence: true,
              length: { minimum: 5 }
end
```

That means that the title should be at least 5 characters in order for the article to go through, otherwise it would not be saved. Now that this rule for your blog is in place, you need to show the blog user that something went wrong and that the form should be filled up properly. To do that, tweak the "create" and "new" actions in app/controllers/articles_controller.rb in order to look like this:

```
def new
  @article = Article.new
end

def create
  @article = Article.new(article_params)

  if @article.save
    redirect_to @article
  else
    render 'new'
  end
end

private
  def article_params
    params.require(:article).permit(:title, :text)
  end
```

What just happened is that you told Rails that if the user did not type in 5 characters in the Title field, it should show the blank form again to the user. That doesn't offer much help. In order to tell the user what went wrong, edit the app/controllers/articles_controller.rb file again and to cater the following changes:

```
def create
  @article = Article.new(article_params)

  if @article.save
    redirect_to @article
  else
```

```
  render 'new'
 end
end

def update
 @article = Article.find(params[:id])

 if @article.update(article_params)
  redirect_to @article
 else
  render 'edit'
 end
end

private
 def article_params
  params.require(:article).permit(:title, :text)
 end
```

Now, to show this to the user, tweak the app/views/articles/index.html.erb file and add the following lines:

```
<table>
 <tr>
  <th>Title</th>
  <th>Text</th>
  <th colspan="2"></th>
 </tr>

 <% @articles.each do |article| %>
  <tr>
   <td><%= article.title %></td>
   <td><%= article.text %></td>
   <td><%= link_to 'Show', article_path(article) %></td>
   <td><%= link_to 'Edit', edit_article_path(article) %></td>
  </tr>
 <% end %>
</table>
```

Chapter 11 Update Articles

You would expect your users to change their minds about the article that they just wrote and make some changes. This would involve the Update action in CRUD, which would prompt you to add an edit action in the ArticlesController and add this function between the "create" and "new" actions. It should look like this:

```
def new
  @article = Article.new
end

def edit
  @article = Article.find(params[:id])
end

def create
  @article = Article.new(article_params)

  if @article.save
    redirect_to @article
  else
    render 'new'
  end
end
```

To allow a view for this, create a file and name it app/views/articles/edit.html.erb and then put in the following lines:

```
<h1>Editing article</h1>

<%= form_for :article, url: article_path(@article), method: :patch do |f| %>

  <% if @article.errors.any? %>
   <div id="error_explanation">
    <h2>
     <%= pluralize(@article.errors.count, "errcr") %> prohibited
     this article from being saved:
    </h2>
    <ul>
     <% @article.errors.full_messages.each do |msg| %>
      <li><%= msg %></li>
     <% end %>
    </ul>
   </div>
  <% end %>
```

```
<p>
 <%= f.label :title %><br>
 <%= f.text_field :title %>
</p>

<p>
 <%= f.label :text %><br>
 <%= f.text_area :text %>
</p>

<p>
 <%= f.submit %>
</p>

<% end %>

<%= link_to 'Back', articles_path %>
```

Now, you would need to create the "update" action in app/controllers/articles_controller.rb. Edit the file to look like this:

```
def create
 @article = Article.new(article_params)

 if @article.save
  redirect_to @article
 else
  render 'new'
 end
end

def update
 @article = Article.find(params[:id])

 if @article.update(article_params)
  redirect_to @article
 else
  render 'edit'
 end
end

private
 def article_params
  params.require(:article).permit(:title, :text)
 end
```

In order to show a link for Edit, you can edit app/views/articles/index.html.erb to make the link appear after the Show link.

```
<table>
 <tr>
  <th>Title</th>
  <th>Text</th>
  <th colspan="2"></th>
 </tr>

 <% @articles.each do |article| %>
  <tr>
   <td><%= article.title %></td>
   <td><%= article.text %></td>
   <td><%= link_to 'Show', article_path(article) %></td>
   <td><%= link_to 'Edit', edit_article_path(article) %></td>
  </tr>
 <% end %>
</table>
```

Now, to give chance for the user to Edit his work, add these lines to the template app/views/articles/show.html.erb:

```
...

<%= link_to 'Back', articles_path %> |
<%= link_to 'Edit', edit_article_path(@article) %>
```

Chapter 12 Destroy Some Data

No, it does not mean that you have to ruin the entire program you built. At this point, you would need to make provisions for the user to delete some of the articles that he wrote. Since you are creating a RESTful program, you would need to use the following route:

DELETE /articles/:id(.:format)   articles#destroy

This route makes it easy for Rails to destroy resources and you would need to make sure that it is placed before the protected or private methods. Let's add this action to the app/controllers/articles_controller.rb file:

```
def destroy
 @article = Article.find(params[:id])
 @article.destroy

 redirect_to articles_path
end
```

After doing so, you would notice that the ArticlesController in app/controllers/articles_controller.rb will now appear this way:

```
class ArticlesController < ApplicationController
 def index
  @articles = Article.all
 end

 def show
  @article = Article.find(params[:id])
 end

 def new
  @article = Article.new
 end

 def edit
  @article = Article.find(params[:id])
 end

 def create
  @article = Article.new(article_params)

  if @article.save
   redirect_to @article
  else
   render 'new'
  end
 end
```

```ruby
def update
  @article = Article.find(params[:id])

  if @article.update(article_params)
    redirect_to @article
  else
    render 'edit'
  end
end

def destroy
  @article = Article.find(params[:id])
  @article.destroy

  redirect_to articles_path
end

private
  def article_params
    params.require(:article).permit(:title, :text)
  end
end
```

Now, it's time for you to let the user know that they have this option. Pull up the app/views/articles/index.html.erb file and add the following lines:

```erb
<h1>Listing Articles</h1>
<%= link_to 'New article', new_article_path %>
<table>
 <tr>
  <th>Title</th>
  <th>Text</th>
  <th colspan="3"></th>
 </tr>

 <% @articles.each do |article| %>
  <tr>
   <td><%= article.title %></td>
   <td><%= article.text %></td>
   <td><%= link_to 'Show', article_path(article) %></td>
   <td><%= link_to 'Edit', edit_article_path(article) %></td>
   <td><%= link_to 'Delete', article_path(article),
       method: :delete,
       data: { confirm: 'Are you sure?' } %></td>
  </tr>
 <% end %>
</table>
```

You would notice that you also added up a feature to make the user confirm whether he really would want to delete the submitted article. Now, in order to make the confirmation box appear, you need to make sure that you have the file jquery_ujs   in   your   machine.

Conclusion

Thank you again for purchasing this book!

I hope this book was able to help you to grasp the basics of Ruby on Rails and allow you to create a webpage based on the codes and processes discussed in this book.

The next step is to discover other applications of the platform and learn other Rails techniques that would improve your program design and integration.

Finally, if you enjoyed this book, please take the time to share your thoughts and post a review on Amazon. We do our best to reach out to readers and provide the best value we can. Your positive review will help us achieve that. It'd be greatly appreciated!

Thank you and good luck!

Check Out My Other Books

Below you'll find some of my other popular books that are popular on Amazon and Kindle as well. Simply click on the links below to check them out. Alternatively, you can visit my author page on Amazon to see other work done by me.

Click here to check out C Programming Success in a Day on Amazon.

Click here to check out Python Programming Success in a Day on Amazon.

Click here to check out PHP Programming Professional Made Easy on Amazon.

Click here to check out HTML Professional Programming Made Easy on Amazon

Click here to check out CSS Programming Professional Made Easy on Amazon.

Click here to check out Windows 8 Tips for Beginners on Amazon.

Click here to check out C Programming Professional Made Easy on Amazon.

Click here to check out JavaScript Programming Made Easy on Amazon

Click here to check out C ++ Programming Success in a Day on Amazon.

Click here to check out the rest of Android Programming in a Day on Amazon.

Click here to check out the rest of Python Programming in a Day on Amazon.

If the links do not work, for whatever reason, you can simply search for these titles on the Amazon website to find them.

www.ingramcontent.com/pod-product-compliance
Lightning Source LLC
Chambersburg PA
CBHW061039050326
40689CB00012B/2892